ECHOES OF TRAGEDY

Piecing Together the Devastating Events
of The New London School Explosion Of
1937 and the Unforgettable Stories of
the Lives Lost on the Darkest Day in
Texas Education History

Angela Morris

Looking Back: Reflections on the New London School Explosion.

Acknowledgments

Before delving into this story, it is important to express our sincere gratitude to everyone who helped make this investigation possible. We owe immense gratitude to the survivors and their families, whose bravery in telling their tales shone light on the darkest corners of the past. This story would not be possible without the tireless efforts of historians, scholars, and archivists who have carefully unearthed forgotten truths and preserved the legacy of the lost. Furthermore, may your trip through these pages commemorate the memories of those who lost their lives and motivate you never to forget. You are the readers who will carry the flame of recollection into the future.

Introduction

Sometimes in life, history leaves scars that never completely heal, ingrained in the collective mind. One such instance is the 1937 New London School Explosion, a tragedy whose aftereffects are still felt decades later due to how terrible and profound it was. In order to comprehend the human cost and resiliency that rose from the ashes, we will piece together the memories in this introduction as we go through the agony and bravery that characterized that tragic day in March.

A Look Back at New London's History

Tucked away in the undulating hills of East Texas, New London first came to light in the early 1900s as a glimmer of promise and opportunity—a thriving center of business and learning that offered future generations a better life. From its modest beginnings as a remote outpost to its development into a bustling community, New London's tale is one of tenacity, inventiveness, and the unwavering pursuit of progress.

Through the haze of time, we catch a glimpse of a vibrant town where the hopes and dreams of its citizens are woven into a tapestry. At the center of this colorful environment rose the London School, a sign of pride and promise, with its halls resonating with the laughter and learning of kids from all walks of life. Beneath the surface of this picture-perfect scene, however, was a silent threat—a ticking time bomb that had the potential to destroy the peace of a spring day and throw an entire neighborhood into darkness.

We shall travel back in time to that tragic morning of March 18, 1937, in the ensuing chapters, following in the footsteps of those whose lives were irrevocably changed by fate and foolishness. We will see firsthand the terrifying explosion, the desperate hunt for survivors among the debris, and the grueling period of grief and recovery that followed. Between the sadness and hopelessness, however, we will also come across stories of fortitude and redemption—of common people achieving great feats in the face of unfathomable misfortune.

As we set out on our historical journey, let's not forget that the New London School Explosion is a real-life example of the resilience of the human spirit, not just a historical account. It is a tale of loss and longing, of grief and consolation, but most of all, it is a tale of hope—a lighthouse that shines through the shadows and tells us that we are never really alone, even in the depths of despair.

PART I: BEFORE THE TRAGEDY

The Birth of New London: A Small Town with Big Dreams

Tucked away in East Texas's lush countryside, New London became a symbol of the pioneering spirit of its forefathers. This quiet village was little more than a collection of log homes strewn among the tall pines in the late 19th century, with dirt roads meandering through maize and cotton fields. However, even in those early years, there was a tangible feeling of promise—a conviction that this little encampment had the capacity to grow into something bigger.

The advent of the railroads in the late 1800s, a pivotal event that revitalized the area and spurred a flood of immigration from far-off places, is credited with giving rise to New London. Aiming to carve out a home for themselves in the wilderness, settlers came to the area, their wagons groaning along dusty routes, drawn by the promise of fertile land and an abundance of lumber. Among them were merchants and farmers, artists and businesspeople, all motivated by a common goal of advancement and success.

With time, New London took shape, becoming a thriving center of trade and culture that gave hope to the surrounding rural areas. The town had a boom beyond anything it had ever seen when oil was discovered in adjacent fields; oilmen and speculators flocked to the town from all over. Brick stores quickly replaced the wooden shanties, and the once-quiet town square was transformed into a hive of trade and business.

But because of the foresight of its civic leaders, New London was not only a center of economic wealth but also a hub of learning and enlightenment. Together, the people of New London built a cutting-edge school building in 1932 that would stand as a testament to the quality of education for future generations. Known as the London School, it was an expansive complex of red-brick buildings set between well-kept lawns and shady woods, a marvel of modern architecture.

The school was as more than simply a place of instruction for the kids of New London; it was a haven, a second home where they could develop and flourish under the careful supervision of committed faculty and staff. Every area of the school brimmed with youthful energy, from the clean pages of textbooks to the boisterous yells of pep rallies, a colorful tapestry of hopes and dreams woven into the fabric of everyday existence.

On March 18, 1937, the sun rose and the people of New London saw a typical day unfold before them: the streets were bustling with the everyday activity, the air crisp with the promise of spring. They had no idea that, before the day was up, their world would undergo an irreversible transformation due to a catastrophe of unfathomable dimensions that was waiting to shattered the peace of their small town life.

The Rise of the London School: From Humble Beginnings to Educational Excellence

Amid the gently undulating hills and whispering pines of East Texas, the London School shone as a beacon of hope and enlightenment in the center of New London. However, the history of this old institution was not one of majesty and extravagance, but rather of the tenacity and resolve of a community committed to giving its kids the greatest education possible.

The London School was founded in the early 1900s when the people of New London realized they needed a state-of-the-art, fully furnished school to meet the demands of their expanding population. During that period, the town had a small number of one-room schoolhouses dispersed over the rural areas, all of which were unable to meet the needs of a fast growing student population.

Inspired by a common goal of advancement and enlightenment, the people of New London united in 1932 to take on a daring project: building a cutting-edge school building that would stand up to any in the area.

Under the direction of a committed team of academics and civic leaders, they combined forces to realize their vision and began construction on a vast campus that would soon become the community's pride.

The London School was founded on the idea that education was the route to a better future for the children of New London, and it represented hope and opportunity for them more than anything else. With its cutting-edge facilities, well-stocked libraries, and contemporary classrooms, the school gave students an unmatched educational experience and gave them the skills they needed to succeed in a world that was changing all the time.

However, the London School's dedication to excellence in all facets of teaching may have been its most noteworthy feature. Every element of the school, from the committed faculty and staff who put in endless effort to motivate and empower their pupils to the demanding curriculum that pushed young brains to new limits of accomplishment, was created to promote a love of learning and an inquiry-based mindset.

The London School's reputation grew throughout time, drawing students from all over the world who wanted to take advantage of its top-notch educational offerings. Within its hallowed halls, students from all origins and walks of life, united by a common desire for knowledge and a dedication to greatness, found a place to call home. These included the offspring of oil barons and the sons and daughters of sharecroppers.

However, the London School was more than simply a hub of academic excellence; it was also a hub of communal life, a gathering place for teachers, parents, and students to share triumphs, lament losses, and create enduring friendships. The school served as a center of community gatherings and a place to build a sense of belonging that went well beyond its boundaries, from band concerts and football games to school dances and picnics.

The London School was a beacon of academic achievement, a tribute to the strength of society, the promise of advancement, and the unwavering spirit of the human pursuit for knowledge, as the sun fell on March 17, 1937, the eve of tragedy. The people of New London had no idea that their cherished school would undergo a permanent transformation, with children's joy no longer filling its halls, but instead their cries of sorrow and despair, before dawn broke on the following day.

Prosperity and Progress: New London in the 1930s

Driven by wealth from the oil fields that dotting the area, New London, Texas saw a thriving and optimistic start to the 1930s. Thanks to the black gold hidden beneath its soil, this small East Texas community found itself well positioned for growth and opportunity while the country struggled with the effects of the Great Depression.

Oil was discovered nearby, and almost immediately afterward, the modest farming village of New London was transformed into a thriving center of industry and trade. Across the countryside, oil derricks sprung up like steel trees, their rhythmic pumps putting a continuous flow of money into the pockets of nearby landowners and business owners. The town's fortunes sprang up with each gusher that emerged from the earth, and goals that had seemed unattainable before now appeared doable.

The oil boom gave the people of New London a renewed sense of opportunity and prosperity. There were plenty of well-paying employment, and the streets were bustling with activity as people arrived from all over the nation to try their luck in the oil fields. A lifeline to families struggling to make ends meet during economic instability, the oil sector offered chances for work at every skill level, from roughnecks to roustabouts, drillers to derrickmen.

However, other areas of the economy also prospered in New London throughout the 1930s, helped along by the influx of capital and wealth that accompanied the oil boom. It wasn't simply the oil business that prospered in the city. Farmers experienced record harvests as a result of advancements in agricultural technology and practices, and local businesses flourished as locals discovered they had more money to spend on products and services.

The town's hopes for the future grew along with its wealth. Inspired by the prosperity of the oil industry and the general optimism of the period, the people of New London banded together in 1932 to take on a monumental project: building a brand-new school building that would stand as a testament to superior education for future generations. Whatever its name, the London School was a symbol of the community's dedication to giving its kids the greatest start in life, regardless of their circumstances or background.

However, there were indications of disaster ahead despite the opulent façade of wealth. A number of difficulties, including social unrest and environmental deterioration, were brought on by the quick speed of development. Concerns over pollution and the depletion of natural resources started to grow as oil firms raced to extract every last drop of crude from the earth, leading to calls for more regulation and control.

Tensions between those who have and those who have not boiled at the same time, causing the town's social fabric to unravel. Some locals profited handsomely from the oil boom, but others were left behind and had to struggle to survive in what appeared to be a hostile economic environment. The community's divisions grew along with the wealth difference, creating the conditions for simmering resentment and discontent.

Nonetheless, the 1930s continued to be a decade of unparalleled expansion and potential for New London, a time characterized by hope, wealth, and advancement despite the difficulties that lay ahead. The town was on the verge of a new age as the decade came to an end, with a bright future ahead of it. Its citizens had no idea that disaster was lurking just around the corner, ready to shatters the peace of their little town life and cast them into the depths of night.

PART II: THE DAY EVERYTHING CHANGED

March 18, 1937: A Normal School Day Begins

New London saw the promise of spring in the air on March 18, 1937. The people of the small East Texas town started their day as usual, not realizing the catastrophe that loomed just over the horizon, as the first rays of sunrise seeped through the pine trees and painted the surroundings in hues of green and gold.

It was just another day for the London School's pupils and faculty, replete with the customs and traditions that had grown ingrained in their way of life. The town was alive with activity as the kids laughed their way to school, their voices mixing with the sound of parents talking and cars humming.

The school's hallowed halls were alive with the vitality of young people as teachers labored hard to instill knowledge and wisdom in their enthusiastic students. Every student, from the tiniest kindergarteners to the oldest seniors in high school, awoke to the day full of expectation and excitement, ready to study and develop in the supportive environment of the London School.

However, beneath the surface of all the fun and education lurked a subtle threat that would soon cause the gullible town to suffer unspeakable destruction. Few people were aware that a lethal buildup of natural gas had been quietly accumulating beneath the school's foundation and silently leaking into the intricate system of pipelines and tunnels concealed below ground.

Maintenance personnel had been trying to fix a leak in the school's heating system that had gone unnoticed for far too long in the weeks preceding that fatal day. In spite of their greatest attempts, the leak's source remained hidden, its existence obscured by the daily commotion and diversions of school.

The stench of gas started to pervade the air as the morning went on and classes started; it was weak at first, but it got stronger every hour. However, the urgent needs of lesson plans and assignments swamped the warning signs, and they were missed in the turmoil of the school day.

The gas had reached a critical point by midmorning, filling the air with its toxic vapors and making the atmosphere within the school oppressive and heavy. Despite the approaching calamity outside their classroom doors, the staff and kids continued their work without raising an alarm or ordering an evacuation.

Then, without warning, the unimaginable occurred: a spark or flicker of flame ignited the flammable gas combination that had built up inside the school. The building burst into a colossal explosion with an overwhelming noise, rocking the quiet of the spring morning and sending shockwaves crashing through the town.

In an instant, the once-proud London School building was reduced to a smoking pile of rubble and trash, forever changing people's lives. As terrified parents and rescuers flocked to the site in a desperate attempt to help those trapped beneath the wreckage, the actual extent of the tragedy became apparent in the ensuing turmoil and uncertainty.

Nevertheless, stories of bravery and altruism emerged among the destruction and hopelessness, as common people stepped up to rescue the lives of others. Amid the darkness of tragedy, the spirit of community and compassion shone brilliantly, from teachers who protected their kids from danger to neighbors who hurried to the help of strangers.

The entire horror of the situation became brutally apparent as the smoke cleared and the dust fell. Over 300 kids and staff members had been killed or seriously injured in an act of recklessness and avarice that had taken their lives. The town of New London would lament its lost innocence in the days and weeks that followed, struggling to come to terms with the terrible truth that disaster may strike at any time and leave destruction in its wake, even in the middle of development and prosperity.

In addition to the sadness and hopelessness, there was a newfound feeling of purpose as well—a resolve to pay tribute to the deceased by making sure that a catastrophe like this would never occur again. A dedication to safety and accountability emerged from the aftermath of the London School explosion, with legislators and educators alike promising to learn from the past and create a better future for future generations.

The Gas Leak: Unseen Danger Lurking Below

On March 18, 1937, as the sun rose over New London, a threat that could not be seen was stealthily making its way through the intricate system of pipes and tunnels that ran beneath the London School. The students and personnel that crowded its hallways had no idea that a lethal buildup of natural gas had been steadily developing and leaking undetected into the building's core.

The gas leak's source can be found a few weeks ago, during an apparently routine school heating system repair. A little leak in one of the school's boilers had gone unreported for far too long, its presence concealed by the everyday commotion and distractions of the school day. Maintenance personnel had been sent to patch the leak.

Despite their best efforts, the staff was unable to locate the leak's source due to the school's outdated infrastructure, which caused several difficulties. The fact that the natural gas used to power the boilers had no color or smell, making it nearly difficult to detect without specialist equipment, further complicated matters.

Days went into weeks, and the leak continued to exist, haunting the area like a ghost while maintenance staff worked nonstop to fix it. However, even as they worked, the threat grew since gas was building up in the cramped areas beneath the school, waiting for a spark to ignite the explosive mixture and cause unthinkable destruction.

Inside the school, meanwhile, things continued as usual as faculty and students went about their regular lives, completely unaware of the silent threat that was waiting to be discovered beneath their feet. With the promise of spring hanging in the air and summer break looming on the horizon, classes were in session, lessons were being taught, and laughter reverberated through the hallways.

However, in the middle of the school day's chaos, there were indications that something was wrong: a slight haze that hung over the classrooms like a veil, and a faint gas smell that persisted in the air. However, these warning indicators were missed in the craziness of the school day, eclipsed by the urgent demands of lesson plans and homework.

As the morning wore on, the gas leak got to the point where it was releasing toxic vapors into the air, making the atmosphere within the school stuffy and unpleasant. Notwithstanding, the staff and students continued their work without raising an alarm or ordering an evacuation, oblivious to the looming catastrophe that was waiting for them within their classrooms.

Then, in an instant, the spark that would eventually ignite the volatile mixture appeared—a flicker of flame, a blast of heat—and all of a sudden, the building shook and trembled with the intensity of the explosion, causing the world to explode in disorder. Walls collapsed, windows broke, and the once-proud London School building was reduced to a smoking pile of debris.

Over 300 kids and staff members were killed or injured in the explosion, their lives cut short by a callous act of incompetence and avarice. The full horror of the situation became brutally evident as the dust fell and the smoke cleared. Families were grieving for their loved ones, and the town of New London was in deep grief as they tried to process how terrible the catastrophe that had befallen them had been.

However, in addition to sadness and misery, the people of New London were incensed and furious, demanding an explanation and responsibility for the lives lost. How could something so tragic have been let to occur? Who was in charge of keeping the facilities of the school maintained? And how could we make sure that a catastrophe like this one never occurred again?

A image of a system that had failed its most vulnerable members emerged as investigators searched through the debris and lawmakers held hearings to get the truth. This system had put profit before safety and had disregarded warning signs until it was too late. The London School explosion left behind a pledge to bring about change, a pledge to make sure that the lessons gained from this catastrophe would not be overlooked and that the lives lost would not have been in vain.

The Explosion: Chaos and Destruction

In New London, Texas, March 18, 1937, started out just like any other day, but it would quickly become known throughout history as a day of unspeakable horror and destruction. With the town bathed in golden light from the rising sun, the London School was a hive of youthful activity, with students laughing and chatting as they got ready for yet another academic day.

Inside the school's maze-like system of pipes and tunnels, a dangerous buildup of natural gas had been quietly accumulating. Those inside its walls were unaware of this silent threat. The gas had gone unnoticed because of the activity of the school day, even though maintenance personnel were trying to fix a leak in the heating system.

As the morning wore on, the gas leak got to the point where it was releasing toxic vapors into the air, making the atmosphere within the school stuffy and unpleasant. Even still, nobody sounded the alarm or issued an evacuation order, and the staff and students carried on with their daily activities, oblivious to the looming catastrophe that was waiting for them within their classrooms.

Then, in an instant, the spark that would eventually ignite the volatile mixture appeared—a flicker of flame, a blast of heat—and all of a sudden, the building shook and trembled with the intensity of the explosion, causing the world to explode in disorder. Walls collapsed, windows broke, and the once-proud London School building was reduced to a smoking pile of debris.

The students and teachers who had filled the school hallways seconds earlier were buried beneath the debris, their aspirations and dreams extinguished in an instant, and lives were permanently altered in the span of a single glance. The smoke billowed into the sky, hiding the sun and descending upon the town of New London, bringing with it a veil of misery.

More than 300 children and staff members lay dead or injured, their bodies buried beneath the twisted wreckage of the school, as the dust settled and the smoke cleared, revealing the whole horror. Families scrambled to find their loved ones amid the chaos and devastation as the town fell into sorrow.

Amid the sorrow and hopelessness, however, were also stories of bravery and sacrifice, as common people stepped up to the plate and put their own lives in danger to rescue those of others. Instructors protected their pupils from injury, neighbors came to the help of strangers, and rescuers put forth endless hours to extract survivors from the debris.

The town of New London struggled to comprehend the extent of the catastrophe that had befallen them as the hours turned into days and the days into weeks. Memorial services were conducted in remembrance of the deceased, inquiries were conducted to ascertain the cause of the accident, and measures were taken to guarantee that a catastrophe of this nature would never occur again.

However, the anguish and suffering of the families who had lost loved ones would never totally go away. They held on to memories of better times—their kids' laughing, their grins' warmth, and the love that had permeated their lives—while they grieved for their kids and their friends.

Thus, on March 18, 1937, as the sun fell, the people of New London stood together in sorrow, connected by a catastrophe that would change their lives forever. Nevertheless, hope persisted among the gloom, as people made plans to rebuild, heal, and pay tribute to the departed by making sure that their legacy would endure in the thoughts and feelings of future generations.

PART III: THE AFTERMATH

The Search for Survivors: Frantic Efforts Amidst the Rubble

The population of New London was plunged into shock and amazement following the disastrous explosion that shook the London School on March 18, 1937. Nevertheless, in the middle of the mayhem and destruction, there emerged a frantic need to locate and save people who were buried beneath the twisted debris.

The sight outside the London School resembled a battlefield when the dust fell and the smoke cleared, with wreckage strewn haphazardly across the school grounds and the air heavy with the pungent smell of gas and smoke. Parents in a panic, rescue personnel, and volunteers arrived at the site, their expressions displaying a mix of dread, resolve, and agony as they started the difficult process of looking for survivors.

Volunteer teams put in endless hours clearing the wreckage and debris that covered the school grounds while the rescue efforts went on unabatedly for hours.

The likelihood of discovering survivors decreased with every second that went by, but the rescuers persisted because they were fervently committed to saving as many lives as they could.

The scene inside the school was one of complete destruction, with the twisted remnants of classrooms and hallways serving as witnesses to the explosion's intensity. Books were strewn around, desks were toppled, and there was a lot of dust and debris in the air. A hand reaching out from under the debris, a faint call for help—signs of life, nevertheless, were visible amid the pandemonium as survivors emerged from the darkness and began to blink in the harsh daylight.

Rescue personnel and volunteers searched every square inch of the debris for signs of life around the clock as the hours went into days, giving the search for survivors a somber urgency. A mixture of terror and hope flooded the air as families held onto hope that their loved ones would somehow survive the destruction.

In addition to the stories of bravery and survival, families also experienced heartache and grief when they learned that their loved ones had died in the explosion. Mothers and fathers, brothers and sisters, wept openly at the loss of those taken from them far too young; their sorrow reverberated through the streets of New London like a dirge of mourning.

However, despite the unfathomable tragedy, the neighborhood's spirit stayed intact as neighbors helped one another out when they needed it. While volunteers toiled nonstop to provide food, housing, and support to those affected by the calamity, churches opened their doors to offer consolation and comfort to the bereaved.

The damage caused by the explosion started to repair as the days turned into weeks, and those weeks into months, but the town's collective memory of that tragic day would always remain marked. The hunt for survivors was seen by the people of New London as a spiritual as well as a physical undertaking, one that would unite them as a group and see them through their darkest moments. Even while the physical wounds would ultimately heal, the tragedy's scars will always serve as a reminder of how fleeting life is and how strong the human spirit can be.

Mourning and Grief: A Community in Shock

The community of New London was left reeling in the wake of the terrible explosion that destroyed the London School on March 18, 1937, with its citizens unable to deal with the intense shock and sadness that followed such a senseless catastrophe. The entire horror of the event became unbearably evident as the smoke and dust fell, shattering many families and plunging a community into darkness. Over 300 lives were lost.

In the turmoil and devastation that followed the explosion, families desperately looked for their loved ones in the haze of agony and shock that characterized those days. Tears were abundant as friends lamented the passing of their classmates and teachers, parents lamented the death of their children, and siblings lamented the loss of their brothers and sisters. The town of New London was in deep mourning as they tried to come to terms with the extent of their loss.

There were, however, brief intervals of optimism and light amid the gloom as the people of New London banded together to help one another out when they needed it. While volunteers toiled nonstop to provide food, housing, and support to those affected by the calamity, churches opened their doors to offer consolation and comfort to the bereaved. In the midst of their shared grief, neighbors reached out to one another, offering a shoulder to weep on, a sympathetic ear, and a consoling embrace.

However, for a great number of people, the tragedy's anguish and heartbreak was unbearable as they grappled with the death of loved ones and the abruptly dashed hopes for the future. Funeral processions made their way through the town's streets, bringing the bodies of the deceased to their final resting places, and the sound of their grief seemed to resound in every corner.

The town of New London united in the days and weeks that followed to pay tribute to the lives and legacies of those lost in the explosion by holding memorials and commemoration rituals. As friends and family shared stories and memories of the ones they had lost, tears mixed with laughter as they took comfort in the knowing that their loved ones would never be forgotten.

New London's citizens, however, were not done with the catastrophe that had befallen them; beneath the surface, there remained a boiling sense of wrath and anger at the deaths of their loved ones. How could something so catastrophic have been permitted to occur? Who was in charge of keeping the facilities of the school maintained? And how could we make sure that a catastrophe like this one never occurred again?

The people of New London pledged to never forget the lessons learnt from the catastrophe while hearings and investigations were conducted to determine the cause of the explosion. Following the London School explosion, both legislators and educators pledged to ensure that the lives lost would not have been in vain. This led to a commitment to safety and accountability.

Thus, the town of New London gradually started to heal as the days grew into weeks and the weeks into months, its wounds acting as a continual reminder of the frailty of life and the resiliency of the human spirit. Even though the tragedy's sorrow would never completely go away, the people of New London took comfort in the fact that they had one another to rely on, support, and get through their darkest moments. The inhabitants of New London confronted the future with a renewed sense of unity, fortitude, and hope, despite the fact that the road to recovery would be difficult and drawn out.

The Toll of Loss: Remembering the Victims

Following the devastating blast that destroyed the London School on March 18, 1937, the town of New London was forced to deal with the enormous amount of loss that had been inflicted upon its residents. The town mourned the loss of innocence and the dashed hopes of a generation, and families lamented the premature deaths of loved ones throughout the sorrowful days that followed.

The full scope of the destruction became agonizingly evident as the smoke and dust fell, taking over 300 lives, a once-thriving school turned to ruins, and a community left reeling in shock and dismay. Parents buried their children, siblings grieved for their brothers and sisters, and friends wept for their professors and classmates— the toll of loss was immense.

Nevertheless, there were glimmer of hope and brightness among the shadows as the people of New London banded together to help one another out when they needed it most. While volunteers toiled nonstop to provide food, housing, and support to those affected by the calamity, churches opened their doors to offer consolation and comfort to the bereaved. In the midst of their shared grief, neighbors reached out to one another, offering a shoulder to weep on, a sympathetic ear, and a consoling embrace.

However, many found it impossible to cope with the unexpected and senseless deaths of their loved ones, making the sorrow of loss unbearable. Funeral processions made their way through the town's streets, bringing the bodies of the deceased to their final resting places, and the sound of their grief seemed to resound in every corner. Families gathered to say their final farewell, memories of happier times filling their brains and their hearts laden with grief, caused tears to fall freely.

Residents of New London wanted to respect the memories of those lost in the explosion, and as the weeks turned into months and the months into years, they found comfort in the act of remembrance. In order to pay homage to the victims' lives and legacies, memorials were built and their names were inscribed in stone. In order to honor the people who had passed away, the community gathered, lay flowers, lighted candles, and said prayers.

However, recounting stories to one another when family and friends gathered to share recollections and anecdotes of the ones they had lost was possibly the most potent gesture of remembrance. They reminisced about the peculiarities and eccentricities that characterized their loved ones through laughter and tears, taking comfort in the idea that their memories would endure in the hearts and minds of those who knew them the best.

The town of New London found strength in the act of recollection as the years went by and the grief of the loss started to lessen. They pledged to never forget the lessons learnt from the catastrophe. A dedication to safety and responsibility emerged from the aftermath of the London School explosion, with legislators and educators striving to guarantee that a catastrophe like this would never occur again.

As the sun sank on yet another day in New London, the town was brought together by a common experience of loss and a shared resolve to pay tribute to the people who had died in the explosion. The people of New London took solace in the idea that their loved ones would live on in the hearts and memories of those who knew and loved them the most, even though the anguish of their absence would never completely go away.

PART IV: SEEKING ANSWERS AND ACCOUNTABILITY

Investigations and Inquiries: Uncovering the Truth Behind the Tragedy

The community of New London was left reeling in the wake of the devastating explosion that tore through the London School on March 18, 1937, with its citizens struggling with shock, grief, and an overwhelming sense of disbelief. But in the middle of all of the turmoil and destruction, there was an overwhelming need for explanations—in the face of such an absurd tragedy, there was an urgent need for justice and accountability.

The town's focus shifted to the challenge of learning the truth about the explosion as legislators and investigators started questions and investigations to ascertain what caused the tragedy as the dust fell and the smoke cleared. What had triggered the explosion-causing gas leak? Who was in charge of keeping the facilities of the school maintained? And was there a way to stop the tragedy?

Teams of specialists started to go through the debris of the London School in an attempt to find information that would help them understand what had happened before the explosion. In an effort to reconstruct the series of events that led to such destruction, investigators painstakingly categorized and examined every item of wreckage and evidence.

The investigation focused on the gas leak that caused the explosion. For weeks before the accident, maintenance staff had been working to plug a leak in the school's heating system that had gone undiscovered for far too long. But what caused the leak in the first place? And why had it taken so long to resolve?

As investigators dug deeper into the circumstances surrounding the maintenance work, a worrying picture of incompetence and oversight by school officials and administrators emerged. Despite multiple complaints from students and staff about the odor of gas in the weeks preceding the explosion, no action was made to investigate or solve the problem—a failing that would have deadly consequences.

However, the guilt did not rest exclusively with the school administration. As the investigation progressed, it became evident that the oil corporations operating in the area shared blame for the accident. In their drive to extract every last drop of oil from the ground, these firms drilled hundreds of wells near the school, resulting in a deadly concentration of natural gas beneath the surface.

As evidence accumulated and the truth began to emerge, New London people wanted justice for those killed in the explosion. Public hearings were convened, witnesses were asked to speak, and lawmakers worked feverishly to pass legislation that would prevent such a catastrophe from happening again.

The investigation's most lasting legacy, however, may be the subsequent dedication to safety and responsibility. The ashes of the London School explosion sparked a renewed desire to guarantee that such a catastrophe never happened again—to hold those responsible accountable and to commemorate the victims' memory by ensuring that their lives were not lost in vain.

As the investigation concluded and the town of New London began the long process of healing and rebuilding, there remained a sense of hope—a hope that from the darkness of tragedy would emerge a brighter future, guided by the lessons learned and the commitment to never forget the lives lost in the pursuit of progress.

Legal Battles: Holding Responsible Parties Accountable

Following the devastating explosion that rocked the London School on March 18, 1937, the town of New London was shattered, with residents dealing with grief, rage, and an overwhelming sense of loss. Despite the damage, there developed a fierce determination to hold those responsible for the disaster accountable—a commitment to justice that would begin a series of judicial fights that would shape the town's future for years.

As the dust fell and the smoke cleared, New London citizens looked to the justice system for answers and accountability. Lawsuits were brought against the school district, local oil corporations, and those in charge of maintaining and overseeing the school's infrastructure. The court struggle that followed would be lengthy and hard, spanning years as families sought justice for the lives killed in the explosion.

The question of culpability was central to the judicial battle: who was ultimately to blame for the disaster that had struck New London? As evidence was produced and people spoke, a distressing picture of incompetence and oversight emerged, involving school authorities, administrators, and oil industry executives.

Despite multiple complaints from students and staff about the odor of gas in the weeks preceding the explosion, no action was made to investigate or solve the problem—a failing that would have deadly consequences. Maintenance personnel had been working to repair a leak in the school's heating system, but their efforts had been impeded by a lack of resources and cooperation from school administrators.

However, the school system was not entirely to blame. As the court struggle progressed, it became evident that the oil firms operating in the area shared blame for the accident. In their drive to extract every last drop of oil from the ground, these firms drilled hundreds of wells near the school, resulting in a deadly concentration of natural gas beneath the surface.

As evidence accumulated and the truth began to emerge, New London people wanted justice for those killed in the explosion. Public hearings were convened, witnesses were asked to speak, and lawmakers worked feverishly to pass legislation that would prevent such a catastrophe from happening again.

But arguably the most lasting effect of the judicial war was the sense of closure and accountability it provided to the municipality of New London. As settlements were agreed and verdicts were delivered, New London residents took comfort in knowing that those responsible for the catastrophe had been held accountable for their acts.

As the court struggle came to an end and the town of New London began the long process of healing and rebuilding, there remained a sense of hope—a hope that out of the darkness of tragedy may arise a brighter future guided by the principles of justice, accountability, and remembering.

Lessons Learned: Safety Reforms and Changes in Education

The devastating explosion that rocked the London School on March 18, 1937, had an enduring impact on the town of New London, Texas. Following the tragic loss of over 300 lives, the community was compelled to face challenging questions about safety, accountability, and the future of education. Chapter 12 dives into the significant lessons learnt from this disaster, the measures put in place to prevent such a tragedy from happening again, and the long-term changes in the educational landscape that emerged from the ashes.

The explosion at the London School served as a wake-up call for the entire nation, highlighting the importance of thorough safety procedures in schools. In the immediate aftermath of the tragedy, municipalities around the country reevaluated their own infrastructure and safety measures, enacting stronger laws to avoid future disasters. Building codes were changed, safety checks were increased, and disaster preparedness procedures were strengthened to safeguard the safety of students and employees.

But the lessons learnt from the New London catastrophe went far beyond physical safety. The explosion triggered a broader discourse about the need of putting kids' well-being and education first. In the years following the accident, educators and legislators alike increased their efforts to build nurturing and supportive learning environments that emphasized not only academic accomplishment but also kids' social, emotional, and physical growth.

One of the most major changes that sprang from the tragedy was a renewed emphasis on transparency and accountability in the educational system. Following the explosion, school districts around the country began instituting mechanisms to guarantee that safety issues were addressed quickly and effectively, and that all stakeholders—students, parents, teachers, and administrators—had a say in the decision-making process.

The catastrophe in New London also sparked technological and infrastructure breakthroughs that would transform the way schools operated. Schools around the country experienced fast remodeling, from the installation of contemporary heating and ventilation systems to the implementation of new safety regulations and emergency response processes, all with the goal of protecting the lives and well-being of students and staff.

The New London tragedy's most lasting consequence, however, was its tremendous impact on American educational culture. In the years following the explosion, educators and policymakers began to appreciate the significance of building inclusive and supportive learning environments that promoted kids' overall development. Schools welcomed innovative teaching methods, put students' well-being first, and highlighted the value of community and participation in the learning process.

The New London tragedy was a watershed moment in the history of American education, sparking a national debate about safety, accountability, and the fundamental ideals that drive our schools. As time passed and the wounds healed, the lessons learnt from this tragedy shaped the way we approached education, inspiring us to strive for quality, equity, and inclusivity in all facets of education.

So, as we reflect on the legacy of the New London tragedy, we are reminded of the human spirit's tenacity and the power of community to overcome even the most difficult circumstances. Though the agony of loss will never go away, the lessons learnt from this tragedy will continue to guide us as we strive to make the world a safer, more egalitarian, and compassionate place for future generations.

PART V: HEALING AND REMEMBERING

Rebuilding Lives: The Journey of Survivors and Families

Following the March 18, 1937, explosion at the New London School, the town of New London, Texas, experienced deep grief and devastation. Families were devastated, lives were permanently changed, and the town was left to deal with the massive loss caused by the horrific occurrence. Chapter 13 delves on the survivors' and families' journeys of survival and perseverance as they attempted to rebuild their lives in the aftermath of the explosion.

In the immediate aftermath of the explosion, survivors and families were confronted with the enormous challenge of picking up the pieces and moving on after such tremendous loss. For those who had lost loved ones, the agony was overwhelming, made worse by the tragedy's sudden and senseless nature. Despite the darkness, there were glimmers of hope—hope for healing, restoration, and a better tomorrow.

For the explosion survivors, the path to rehabilitation was long and difficult, with physical injuries, emotional scars, and persistent anguish. Many endured months, if not years, of rehabilitation and therapy as they attempted to cope with the event's devastation and the loss of friends and classmates. However, with the help of their families, communities, and their own resilience, they gradually began to reconstruct their lives, finding strength in the knowledge that they were not alone in their battle.

For the families who had lost loved ones in the explosion, the grieving process was difficult and painful. Every day was a battle against grief as they dealt with the tremendous void left by the loss of their loved ones. But, in the middle of the tears and sadness, there were moments of comfort—memories shared, stories told, and the knowing that their loved ones would live on in the hearts and minds of those closest to them.

As the months and years passed and the wounds of the past began to heal, the survivors and families of the New London School explosion found strength in their shared experiences and desire to memorialize those who died in the disaster. Memorials were built, scholarships were made, and community events were held to honor the victims and ensure that their memory would never be forgotten.

But arguably the most potent type of healing came from within—the human spirit's tenacity, ability for forgiveness, and resolve to find meaning in the midst of tragedy. As survivors and families banded together to help one another in their time of need, they found comfort in the links of community and the knowledge that they were not alone in their grief.

As time passed and the scars of the past faded, the survivors and families of the New London School explosion found hope in the promise of a better future— a future built on recollection, resilience, and the enduring strength of the human spirit. Though the agony of loss will never go away, the survivors' and families' journey of healing and rebuilding following the New London School explosion demonstrates the resilience of the human spirit and the ability to hope in the face of adversity.

Following the devastating New London School explosion on March 18, 1937, the town of New London, Texas, was left reeling from the destruction caused by the deaths of over 300 people. As the community dealt with loss and attempted to heal in the aftermath of the accident, the urge to commemorate and remember the fallen became increasingly important. Chapter 14 looks into the deep efforts made to honor the victims of the explosion, including the installation of memorials, tributes, and the lasting legacy of remembrance that resulted from the catastrophe.

The town of New London was flooded with grief in the immediate wake of the explosion, as families lamented the loss of loved ones and the community banded together to help one another in their hour of crisis. Despite the agony and loss, there was a communal commitment to respect the memory of those who died in the tragedy—to guarantee that their lives were not forgotten and that their legacies would live on for future generations.

One of the first steps in commemorating the departed was to build memorials to their memory. In the days and weeks after the explosion, improvised shrines arose throughout the town, filled with flowers, candles, and photographs of the victims. These spontaneous tributes acted as a focal point for the community's loss, providing an opportunity for introspection, remembering, and collective mourning.

However, as time passed and the wounds of the past healed, the necessity for more permanent memorials became clear. In the years since the explosion, attempts have been made to establish permanent monuments to the victims, ensuring that their legacy be perpetuated for future generations. Memorials were created in parks, schools, and public locations around the town, each one a testimony to the fallen's lasting legacy.

One of the most famous memorials to arise from the disaster was the New London School Memorial Arch, which was built in 1939 to honor the victims' memories while also serving as a symbol of hope and resilience for the town. Standing tall and proud, the arch served as a symbol of the town's strength and solidarity in the face of tragedy, as well as a light of hope for the future.

In addition to physical memorials, a variety of tributes were erected to memorialize the victims' memories in the years following the explosion. Scholarships were created in their honor, providing financial assistance to students pursuing their educational ambitions. Annual community events and fundraisers were arranged to raise awareness and celebrate the tragedy's anniversary, ensuring that the memory of the lost was never forgotten by the town.

Perhaps the most enduring impact of the New London School explosion is the sense of memory that still pervades the town today. Though the agony of loss will never go away completely, people of New London can take consolation in knowing that the memory of the fallen lives on in the hearts and thoughts of those who knew and loved them best. Through memorials, tributes, and acts of memory, the town of New London ensures that the victims' legacy lives on for future generations, serving as a reminder of the human spirit's tenacity and the power of community in the face of tragedy.

The Legacy of New London: Impacts on Education and Safety

The New London School explosion on March 18, 1937, is remembered as one of the saddest days in American educational history. The disaster not only killed over 300 students and teachers, but it also sent shockwaves across the country, prompting a renewed focus on school safety and leaving an everlasting effect on the educational landscape. Chapter 15 dives into the New London School explosion's long-term influence on education and safety, as well as the lessons learnt from the catastrophe.

The explosion at the New London School was a watershed moment in educational history, highlighting the critical need for adequate safety precautions in schools. Following the incident, municipalities around the country reevaluated their own infrastructure and safety measures, enacting stronger restrictions to prevent future disasters. Building codes were changed, safety checks were increased, and disaster preparedness procedures were strengthened to safeguard the safety of students and employees.

But New London's legacy stretches far beyond physical safety. The tragedy generated a broader discourse about the significance of putting children' well-being and education first. In the years after the explosion, educators and legislators increased their efforts to provide loving and supportive learning environments, concentrating not only on academic accomplishment but also on students' social, emotional, and physical well-being.

One of the most notable aftereffects of the New London School explosion was a renewed emphasis on transparency and accountability in education. Following the tragedy, school districts around the country began instituting procedures to guarantee that safety concerns were addressed quickly and effectively, and that all stakeholders—students, parents, teachers, and administrators—had a say in decision-making processes.

The catastrophe also prompted technological and infrastructure breakthroughs that would transform how schools operated. Schools underwent fast modernization, from the installation of contemporary heating and ventilation systems to the implementation of new safety regulations and emergency response processes, all with the goal of protecting students' and staff members' lives and well-being.

The New London School explosion's most lasting legacy, however, was its tremendous impact on American educational culture. In the years since the tragedy, educators and policymakers have recognized the significance of fostering inclusive and supportive learning environments that promote kids' complete development. Schools welcomed innovative teaching methods, put students' well-being first, and highlighted the value of community and participation in the learning process.

The legacy of New London stands as a reminder of the human spirit's tenacity and the power of community to overcome even the most difficult circumstances. Though the agony of loss will never go away, the lessons learned from the tragedy continue to affect how we approach education, encouraging us to strive for quality, equity, and inclusivity in all aspects of learning. As we reflect on the aftermath of the New London School explosion, we are reminded of the significance of vigilance, compassion, and solidarity in achieving a safer and more equitable future for all.

Conclusion

Looking Back: Reflections on the New London School Explosion.

As we think on the awful events of March 18, 1937, and the devastating consequences of the New London School explosion, we cannot help but feel tremendous regret and loss. The lives lost, the dreams left unfulfilled, and the communities forever changed by the catastrophe serve as a sobering reminder of the fragility of life and the unpredictable nature of fate. Despite the darkness, there are moments of light—acts of courage, acts of generosity, and the eternal tenacity of the human spirit—that serve as beacons of hope in the face of disaster.

The New London School explosion was a tragedy of epic dimensions, shaking the town's foundations and sending shockwaves across the nation. Families were shattered, lives were permanently altered, and a community was left to deal with the immense sadness and loss that resulted. Even at the darkest of times, there were moments of heroism and compassion—neighbors assisting neighbors, strangers banding together in support, and a community determined to succeed.

As we reflect on the events of that sad day, we are reminded of the importance of remembrance—the need to commemorate the memory of those who died in the explosion and ensure that their legacy goes on in the hearts and minds of subsequent generations. Memorials and memorials serve as physical reminders of the lives lost and sacrifices made, whilst community activities and rituals allow for contemplation and healing. We pay tribute to the past by doing acts of remembering, ensuring that the lessons learned from the catastrophe are never forgotten.

Even while we lament the loss of those who left us too soon, we must take solace in knowing that their lives were not in vain. The New London School explosion left a lasting legacy of safety, accountability, and the significance of putting kids' well-being first. In the years since the explosion, communities around the country have established tougher safety standards, renovated school facilities, and prioritized students' holistic development, ensuring that such a catastrophe never occurs again.

Moving Forward: Lessons for the Future

As we look to the future, we must remember the lessons from the New London School explosion and be diligent in our efforts to provide safe, supporting, and nurturing learning environments for all students. The tragedy serves as a sharp reminder of the dangers of negligence, complacency, and failing to prioritize the safety and well-being of people in our care. We must never forget the lives lost in the explosion, nor the sacrifices made by survivors and families who continue to face the consequences of the catastrophe.

Moving forward, we must remain committed to creating a culture of safety, accountability, and compassion in our schools—a culture that prioritizes the lives and well-being of all students and staff. We must prioritize identifying and mitigating safety threats, implementing complete emergency preparedness plans, and creating inclusive and supportive learning environments that allow kids to succeed academically, socially, and emotionally.

But, most importantly, we must never lose sight of the human element—the faces behind the statistics, the tales behind the headlines, and the lives forever altered by the March 18, 1937 disaster. As we move forward, let us remember those who died in the explosion and honor their legacy by working relentlessly to prevent such a catastrophe from occurring again. This way, we honor the past while also ensuring the future for future generations.

www.ingramcontent.com/pod-product-compliance
Lightning Source LLC
Chambersburg PA
CBHW050825250726
48653CB00006B/2435